50 Creative Cupcake Recipes

By: Kelly Johnson

Table of Contents

- Chocolate Peanut Butter Cupcakes
- Lemon Raspberry Cupcakes
- Cookies and Cream Cupcakes
- Salted Caramel Pretzel Cupcakes
- Matcha Green Tea Cupcakes
- Churro Cupcakes with Cinnamon Frosting
- S'mores Cupcakes
- Maple Bacon Cupcakes
- Piña Colada Cupcakes
- Red Velvet Cheesecake Cupcakes
- Strawberry Shortcake Cupcakes
- Espresso Mocha Cupcakes
- Black Forest Cupcakes
- Funfetti Birthday Cupcakes
- Honey Lavender Cupcakes
- Caramel Apple Cupcakes
- Chocolate Mint Cupcakes
- Peanut Butter and Jelly Cupcakes
- Pumpkin Spice Latte Cupcakes
- Almond Joy Cupcakes
- Lemon Blueberry Cupcakes
- Tiramisu Cupcakes
- Coconut Lime Cupcakes
- Cherry Almond Cupcakes
- Gingerbread Cupcakes with Eggnog Frosting
- Neapolitan Cupcakes
- Chocolate Cherry Cola Cupcakes
- Mango Coconut Cupcakes
- Champagne Cupcakes
- Rocky Road Cupcakes
- Brownie Batter Cupcakes
- Piñata Surprise Cupcakes
- White Chocolate Raspberry Cupcakes
- Dark Chocolate Chili Cupcakes
- Watermelon Cupcakes

- Pistachio Rose Cupcakes
- Carrot Cake Cupcakes with Cream Cheese Frosting
- Peanut Butter Banana Cupcakes
- Chocolate Coconut Cupcakes
- Lemon Meringue Cupcakes
- Blueberry Pancake Cupcakes
- Mocha Almond Fudge Cupcakes
- Cotton Candy Cupcakes
- Blackberry Basil Cupcakes
- Snickerdoodle Cupcakes
- Butterbeer Cupcakes
- Hazelnut Praline Cupcakes
- Raspberry Champagne Cupcakes
- Banana Foster Cupcakes
- Chocolate Guinness Cupcakes

Chocolate Peanut Butter Cupcakes

Ingredients:

- 1 cup flour
- ½ cup cocoa powder
- 1 tsp baking powder
- ½ tsp salt
- ½ cup butter, softened
- ¾ cup sugar
- 2 eggs
- ½ cup milk
- ½ cup peanut butter
- 12 mini peanut butter cups

Instructions:

1. Preheat oven to 350°F.
2. Mix dry ingredients; separately, beat butter, sugar, and eggs.
3. Combine and stir in milk.
4. Fill cupcake liners halfway, add a peanut butter cup, and cover.
5. Bake for 18 minutes.

Lemon Raspberry Cupcakes

Ingredients:

- 1 ½ cups flour
- 1 tsp baking powder
- ½ tsp salt
- ½ cup butter
- ¾ cup sugar
- 2 eggs
- Zest of 1 lemon
- ½ cup buttermilk
- ½ cup fresh raspberries

Instructions:

1. Preheat oven to 350°F.
2. Beat butter, sugar, eggs, and lemon zest.
3. Mix dry ingredients and add alternately with buttermilk.
4. Fold in raspberries and bake for 20 minutes.

Cookies and Cream Cupcakes

Ingredients:

- 1 cup flour
- ½ tsp baking powder
- ½ cup butter
- ¾ cup sugar
- 2 eggs
- ½ cup milk
- 10 crushed Oreos

Instructions:

1. Preheat oven to 350°F.
2. Mix dry ingredients; separately, beat butter, sugar, and eggs.
3. Combine and fold in crushed Oreos.
4. Bake for 18 minutes.

Salted Caramel Pretzel Cupcakes

Ingredients:

- 1 ½ cups flour
- 1 tsp baking powder
- ½ cup butter
- ¾ cup brown sugar
- 2 eggs
- ½ cup milk
- ¼ cup caramel sauce
- Crushed pretzels for topping

Instructions:

1. Preheat oven to 350°F.
2. Beat butter and sugar, then add eggs.
3. Mix dry ingredients and add with milk.
4. Fill liners, drizzle caramel, and bake for 18 minutes.
5. Top with pretzels.

Matcha Green Tea Cupcakes

Ingredients:

- 1 cup flour
- 1 tsp baking powder
- ½ cup sugar
- 2 tsp matcha powder
- ½ cup butter
- 2 eggs
- ½ cup milk

Instructions:

1. Preheat oven to 350°F.
2. Mix dry ingredients.
3. Beat butter and sugar, then add eggs.
4. Combine with dry mix and bake for 18 minutes.

Churro Cupcakes with Cinnamon Frosting

Ingredients:

- 1 cup flour
- 1 tsp baking powder
- ½ cup sugar
- 1 tsp cinnamon
- ½ cup butter
- 2 eggs
- ½ cup milk

Instructions:

1. Preheat oven to 350°F.
2. Mix dry ingredients.
3. Beat butter and sugar, then add eggs.
4. Fill liners, bake for 18 minutes, and top with cinnamon frosting.

S'mores Cupcakes

Ingredients:

- 1 cup flour
- ½ cup cocoa powder
- 1 tsp baking powder
- ½ cup butter
- ¾ cup sugar
- 2 eggs
- ½ cup milk
- ½ cup crushed graham crackers
- Marshmallow frosting

Instructions:

1. Preheat oven to 350°F.
2. Mix dry ingredients.
3. Beat butter and sugar, then add eggs.
4. Fold in graham crackers, bake for 18 minutes, and top with marshmallow frosting.

Maple Bacon Cupcakes

Ingredients:

- 1 ½ cups flour
- 1 tsp baking powder
- ½ cup butter
- ¾ cup maple syrup
- 2 eggs
- ½ cup milk
- ½ cup cooked bacon, crumbled

Instructions:

1. Preheat oven to 350°F.
2. Beat butter and syrup, then add eggs.
3. Mix dry ingredients and add with milk.
4. Fold in bacon and bake for 18 minutes.

Piña Colada Cupcakes

Ingredients:

- 1 cup flour
- 1 tsp baking powder
- ½ cup sugar
- ½ cup butter
- 2 eggs
- ½ cup coconut milk
- ½ cup crushed pineapple

Instructions:

1. Preheat oven to 350°F.
2. Mix dry ingredients.
3. Beat butter and sugar, then add eggs.
4. Fold in coconut milk and pineapple, bake for 18 minutes.

Red Velvet Cheesecake Cupcakes

Ingredients:

- 1 cup flour
- 1 tsp cocoa powder
- ½ tsp baking powder
- ½ cup butter
- ¾ cup sugar
- 2 eggs
- ½ cup buttermilk
- 1 tbsp red food coloring
- ½ cup cream cheese filling

Instructions:

1. Preheat oven to 350°F.
2. Mix dry ingredients.
3. Beat butter and sugar, then add eggs and food coloring.
4. Fill liners halfway, add cream cheese filling, and cover.
5. Bake for 20 minutes.

Strawberry Shortcake Cupcakes

Ingredients:

- 1 ½ cups flour
- 1 tsp baking powder
- ½ cup butter
- ¾ cup sugar
- 2 eggs
- ½ cup milk
- ½ cup diced strawberries
- Whipped cream & sliced strawberries for topping

Instructions:

1. Preheat oven to 350°F.
2. Beat butter and sugar, then add eggs.
3. Mix dry ingredients and add alternately with milk.
4. Fold in strawberries, bake for 18 minutes, and top with whipped cream.

Espresso Mocha Cupcakes

Ingredients:

- 1 cup flour
- ½ cup cocoa powder
- 1 tsp baking powder
- ½ cup sugar
- ½ cup butter
- 2 eggs
- ¼ cup espresso
- ¼ cup milk
- Chocolate ganache for topping

Instructions:

1. Preheat oven to 350°F.
2. Beat butter and sugar, then add eggs.
3. Mix dry ingredients and add espresso & milk.
4. Bake for 18 minutes and top with ganache.

Black Forest Cupcakes

Ingredients:

- 1 cup flour
- ½ cup cocoa powder
- 1 tsp baking powder
- ½ cup sugar
- ½ cup butter
- 2 eggs
- ½ cup milk
- ½ cup cherry pie filling
- Whipped cream & chocolate shavings

Instructions:

1. Preheat oven to 350°F.
2. Beat butter and sugar, then add eggs.
3. Mix dry ingredients and add with milk.
4. Fill liners, add cherry filling, and bake for 18 minutes.
5. Top with whipped cream and chocolate shavings.

Funfetti Birthday Cupcakes

Ingredients:

- 1 ½ cups flour
- 1 tsp baking powder
- ½ cup sugar
- ½ cup butter
- 2 eggs
- ½ cup milk
- ½ cup rainbow sprinkles

Instructions:

1. Preheat oven to 350°F.
2. Beat butter and sugar, then add eggs.
3. Mix dry ingredients and add milk.
4. Fold in sprinkles and bake for 18 minutes.

Honey Lavender Cupcakes

Ingredients:

- 1 ½ cups flour
- 1 tsp baking powder
- ½ cup butter
- ¾ cup sugar
- 2 eggs
- ½ cup milk
- 1 tbsp dried lavender
- ¼ cup honey

Instructions:

1. Preheat oven to 350°F.
2. Heat milk with lavender, let steep, and strain.
3. Beat butter, sugar, eggs, and honey.
4. Mix dry ingredients and add with milk.
5. Bake for 18 minutes.

Caramel Apple Cupcakes

Ingredients:

- 1 ½ cups flour
- 1 tsp baking powder
- ½ cup sugar
- ½ cup butter
- 2 eggs
- ½ cup milk
- ½ cup diced apples
- ¼ cup caramel sauce

Instructions:

1. Preheat oven to 350°F.
2. Beat butter and sugar, then add eggs.
3. Mix dry ingredients and add with milk.
4. Fold in apples, bake for 18 minutes, and drizzle caramel.

Chocolate Mint Cupcakes

Ingredients:

- 1 cup flour
- ½ cup cocoa powder
- 1 tsp baking powder
- ½ cup sugar
- ½ cup butter
- 2 eggs
- ½ cup milk
- 1 tsp peppermint extract
- Chocolate chips for topping

Instructions:

1. Preheat oven to 350°F.
2. Beat butter and sugar, then add eggs.
3. Mix dry ingredients and add milk & peppermint.
4. Bake for 18 minutes and top with chocolate chips.

Peanut Butter and Jelly Cupcakes

Ingredients:

- 1 ½ cups flour
- 1 tsp baking powder
- ½ cup sugar
- ½ cup butter
- 2 eggs
- ½ cup milk
- ¼ cup peanut butter
- ¼ cup jam

Instructions:

1. Preheat oven to 350°F.
2. Beat butter and sugar, then add eggs and peanut butter.
3. Mix dry ingredients and add with milk.
4. Fill liners, add jam, and bake for 18 minutes.

Pumpkin Spice Latte Cupcakes

Ingredients:

- 1 ½ cups flour
- 1 tsp baking powder
- ½ cup sugar
- ½ cup butter
- 2 eggs
- ½ cup pumpkin puree
- ¼ cup brewed coffee
- 1 tsp pumpkin spice

Instructions:

1. Preheat oven to 350°F.
2. Beat butter and sugar, then add eggs and pumpkin.
3. Mix dry ingredients and add with coffee.
4. Bake for 18 minutes and top with whipped cream.

Almond Joy Cupcakes

Ingredients:

- 1 cup flour
- ½ cup cocoa powder
- 1 tsp baking powder
- ½ cup sugar
- ½ cup butter
- 2 eggs
- ½ cup coconut milk
- ¼ cup chopped almonds
- ½ cup shredded coconut

Instructions:

1. Preheat oven to 350°F.
2. Beat butter and sugar, then add eggs.
3. Mix dry ingredients and add coconut milk.
4. Fold in almonds & coconut, bake for 18 minutes.

Lemon Blueberry Cupcakes

Ingredients:

- 1 ½ cups flour
- 1 tsp baking powder
- ½ cup butter
- ¾ cup sugar
- 2 eggs
- ½ cup milk
- 1 tbsp lemon zest
- ½ cup fresh blueberries

Instructions:

1. Preheat oven to 350°F.
2. Beat butter and sugar, then add eggs and lemon zest.
3. Mix dry ingredients and add alternately with milk.
4. Fold in blueberries, bake for 18 minutes, and top with lemon frosting.

Tiramisu Cupcakes

Ingredients:

- 1 ½ cups flour
- 1 tsp baking powder
- ½ cup butter
- ¾ cup sugar
- 2 eggs
- ½ cup milk
- ¼ cup brewed espresso
- ½ cup mascarpone cheese
- Cocoa powder for dusting

Instructions:

1. Preheat oven to 350°F.
2. Beat butter and sugar, then add eggs.
3. Mix dry ingredients and add milk and espresso.
4. Bake for 18 minutes, top with mascarpone frosting, and dust with cocoa powder.

Coconut Lime Cupcakes

Ingredients:

- 1 ½ cups flour
- 1 tsp baking powder
- ½ cup sugar
- ½ cup butter
- 2 eggs
- ½ cup coconut milk
- 1 tbsp lime zest
- ½ cup shredded coconut

Instructions:

1. Preheat oven to 350°F.
2. Beat butter and sugar, then add eggs.
3. Mix dry ingredients and add coconut milk and lime zest.
4. Fold in shredded coconut and bake for 18 minutes.

Cherry Almond Cupcakes

Ingredients:

- 1 ½ cups flour
- 1 tsp baking powder
- ½ cup sugar
- ½ cup butter
- 2 eggs
- ½ cup milk
- ¼ cup chopped cherries
- 1 tsp almond extract

Instructions:

1. Preheat oven to 350°F.
2. Beat butter and sugar, then add eggs and almond extract.
3. Mix dry ingredients and add with milk.
4. Fold in cherries and bake for 18 minutes.

Gingerbread Cupcakes with Eggnog Frosting

Ingredients:

- 1 ½ cups flour
- 1 tsp baking powder
- ½ cup sugar
- ½ cup molasses
- ½ cup butter
- 2 eggs
- ½ cup milk
- 1 tsp ground ginger
- 1 tsp cinnamon
- Eggnog frosting for topping

Instructions:

1. Preheat oven to 350°F.
2. Beat butter, sugar, and molasses, then add eggs.
3. Mix dry ingredients and add with milk.
4. Bake for 18 minutes and top with eggnog frosting.

Neapolitan Cupcakes

Ingredients:

- 1 cup flour
- ½ tsp baking powder
- ½ cup sugar
- ½ cup butter
- 2 eggs
- ¼ cup milk
- ¼ cup cocoa powder
- 1 tsp vanilla extract
- ½ cup strawberry puree

Instructions:

1. Preheat oven to 350°F.
2. Divide batter into three bowls:
    - One plain vanilla.
    - One with cocoa powder.
    - One with strawberry puree.
3. Layer each flavor into liners and bake for 18 minutes.

Chocolate Cherry Cola Cupcakes

Ingredients:

- 1 cup flour
- ½ cup cocoa powder
- 1 tsp baking powder
- ½ cup sugar
- ½ cup butter
- 2 eggs
- ½ cup cherry cola
- ½ cup chopped cherries

Instructions:

1. Preheat oven to 350°F.
2. Beat butter and sugar, then add eggs.
3. Mix dry ingredients and add cherry cola.
4. Fold in cherries, bake for 18 minutes, and top with chocolate frosting.

Mango Coconut Cupcakes

Ingredients:

- 1 ½ cups flour
- 1 tsp baking powder
- ½ cup sugar
- ½ cup butter
- 2 eggs
- ½ cup coconut milk
- ½ cup diced mango
- ¼ cup shredded coconut

Instructions:

1. Preheat oven to 350°F.
2. Beat butter and sugar, then add eggs.
3. Mix dry ingredients and add coconut milk.
4. Fold in mango and coconut, then bake for 18 minutes.

Champagne Cupcakes

Ingredients:

- 1 ½ cups flour
- 1 tsp baking powder
- ½ cup sugar
- ½ cup butter
- 2 eggs
- ½ cup champagne

Instructions:

1. Preheat oven to 350°F.
2. Beat butter and sugar, then add eggs.
3. Mix dry ingredients and add champagne.
4. Bake for 18 minutes and top with champagne frosting.

Rocky Road Cupcakes

Ingredients:

- 1 cup flour
- ½ cup cocoa powder
- 1 tsp baking powder
- ½ cup sugar
- ½ cup butter
- 2 eggs
- ½ cup milk
- ½ cup chopped nuts
- ½ cup mini marshmallows
- ¼ cup chocolate chips

Instructions:

1. Preheat oven to 350°F.
2. Beat butter and sugar, then add eggs.
3. Mix dry ingredients and add milk.
4. Fold in nuts, marshmallows, and chocolate chips.
5. Bake for 18 minutes and top with marshmallow frosting.

Brownie Batter Cupcakes

Ingredients:

- 1 ½ cups flour
- ½ cup cocoa powder
- 1 tsp baking powder
- ½ cup sugar
- ½ cup butter
- 2 eggs
- ½ cup milk
- ½ cup brownie batter

Instructions:

1. Preheat oven to 350°F.
2. Beat butter and sugar, then add eggs.
3. Mix dry ingredients and add milk.
4. Fill cupcake liners halfway, add a spoonful of brownie batter, then top with more batter.
5. Bake for 18 minutes and top with chocolate ganache.

Piñata Surprise Cupcakes
Ingredients:

- 1 ½ cups flour
- 1 tsp baking powder
- ½ cup sugar
- ½ cup butter
- 2 eggs
- ½ cup milk
- ½ cup mini M&Ms or sprinkles for filling

Instructions:

1. Preheat oven to 350°F.
2. Beat butter and sugar, then add eggs.
3. Mix dry ingredients and add milk.
4. Bake for 18 minutes.
5. Once cooled, cut out the center and fill with M&Ms, then top with frosting.

White Chocolate Raspberry Cupcakes
Ingredients:

- 1 ½ cups flour
- 1 tsp baking powder
- ½ cup sugar
- ½ cup butter
- 2 eggs
- ½ cup milk
- ½ cup fresh raspberries
- ½ cup melted white chocolate

Instructions:

1. Preheat oven to 350°F.
2. Beat butter and sugar, then add eggs.
3. Mix dry ingredients and add milk.
4. Fold in raspberries and melted white chocolate.
5. Bake for 18 minutes and top with white chocolate frosting.

Dark Chocolate Chili Cupcakes
Ingredients:

- 1 ½ cups flour
- ½ cup cocoa powder
- 1 tsp baking powder
- ½ cup sugar
- ½ cup butter
- 2 eggs
- ½ cup milk
- ½ tsp cayenne pepper

Instructions:

1. Preheat oven to 350°F.
2. Beat butter and sugar, then add eggs.
3. Mix dry ingredients and add milk.
4. Bake for 18 minutes and top with dark chocolate ganache.

Watermelon Cupcakes

Ingredients:

- 1 ½ cups flour
- 1 tsp baking powder
- ½ cup sugar
- ½ cup butter
- 2 eggs
- ½ cup milk
- ½ tsp watermelon extract
- Pink food coloring
- Mini chocolate chips

Instructions:

1. Preheat oven to 350°F.
2. Beat butter and sugar, then add eggs.
3. Mix dry ingredients and add milk and watermelon extract.
4. Add pink food coloring and fold in mini chocolate chips.
5. Bake for 18 minutes and top with green-tinted frosting.

Pistachio Rose Cupcakes
Ingredients:

- 1 ½ cups flour
- 1 tsp baking powder
- ½ cup sugar
- ½ cup butter
- 2 eggs
- ½ cup milk
- ¼ cup ground pistachios
- ½ tsp rose water

Instructions:

1. Preheat oven to 350°F.
2. Beat butter and sugar, then add eggs.
3. Mix dry ingredients and add milk and rose water.
4. Fold in ground pistachios and bake for 18 minutes.
5. Top with rose-infused buttercream and crushed pistachios.

Carrot Cake Cupcakes with Cream Cheese Frosting
Ingredients:

- 1 ½ cups flour
- 1 tsp baking powder
- ½ cup sugar
- ½ cup butter
- 2 eggs
- ½ cup grated carrots
- ½ tsp cinnamon
- ½ cup chopped walnuts

Instructions:

1. Preheat oven to 350°F.
2. Beat butter and sugar, then add eggs.
3. Mix dry ingredients and fold in carrots and walnuts.
4. Bake for 18 minutes and top with cream cheese frosting.

Peanut Butter Banana Cupcakes

Ingredients:

- 1 ½ cups flour
- 1 tsp baking powder
- ½ cup sugar
- ½ cup butter
- 2 eggs
- ½ cup mashed banana
- ½ cup peanut butter

Instructions:

1. Preheat oven to 350°F.
2. Beat butter and sugar, then add eggs.
3. Mix dry ingredients and add mashed banana and peanut butter.
4. Bake for 18 minutes and top with peanut butter frosting.

Chocolate Coconut Cupcakes

Ingredients:

- 1 ½ cups flour
- ½ cup cocoa powder
- 1 tsp baking powder
- ½ cup sugar
- ½ cup butter
- 2 eggs
- ½ cup coconut milk
- ½ cup shredded coconut

Instructions:

1. Preheat oven to 350°F.
2. Beat butter and sugar, then add eggs.
3. Mix dry ingredients and add coconut milk.
4. Fold in shredded coconut and bake for 18 minutes.
5. Top with chocolate ganache and toasted coconut flakes.

Lemon Meringue Cupcakes
Ingredients:

- 1 ½ cups flour
- 1 tsp baking powder
- ½ cup sugar
- ½ cup butter
- 2 eggs
- ½ cup lemon juice
- 1 tbsp lemon zest
- Meringue topping

Instructions:

1. Preheat oven to 350°F.
2. Beat butter and sugar, then add eggs.
3. Mix dry ingredients and add lemon juice and zest.
4. Bake for 18 minutes.
5. Top with meringue and toast with a torch.

Blueberry Pancake Cupcakes

Ingredients:

- 1 ½ cups flour
- 1 tsp baking powder
- ½ cup sugar
- ½ cup butter
- 2 eggs
- ½ cup buttermilk
- ½ cup fresh blueberries
- 1 tsp vanilla
- Maple syrup for drizzle

Instructions:

1. Preheat oven to 350°F.
2. Cream butter and sugar, then add eggs and vanilla.
3. Mix dry ingredients and add buttermilk.
4. Fold in blueberries and bake for 18 minutes.
5. Top with maple frosting and a drizzle of maple syrup.

Mocha Almond Fudge Cupcakes

Ingredients:

- 1 ½ cups flour
- ½ cup cocoa powder
- 1 tsp baking powder
- ½ cup sugar
- ½ cup butter
- 2 eggs
- ½ cup brewed coffee
- ½ cup chopped almonds

Instructions:

1. Preheat oven to 350°F.
2. Beat butter and sugar, then add eggs.
3. Mix dry ingredients and add brewed coffee.
4. Fold in almonds and bake for 18 minutes.
5. Top with mocha frosting and chocolate drizzle.

Cotton Candy Cupcakes
Ingredients:

- 1 ½ cups flour
- 1 tsp baking powder
- ½ cup sugar
- ½ cup butter
- 2 eggs
- ½ cup milk
- ½ tsp cotton candy extract
- Pink and blue food coloring

Instructions:

1. Preheat oven to 350°F.
2. Cream butter and sugar, then add eggs.
3. Mix dry ingredients and add milk and cotton candy extract.
4. Divide batter into two bowls, tint one pink and one blue.
5. Swirl together and bake for 18 minutes.
6. Top with cotton candy frosting and sprinkles.

Blackberry Basil Cupcakes

Ingredients:

- 1 ½ cups flour
- 1 tsp baking powder
- ½ cup sugar
- ½ cup butter
- 2 eggs
- ½ cup milk
- ½ cup fresh blackberries
- 1 tsp chopped basil

Instructions:

1. Preheat oven to 350°F.
2. Beat butter and sugar, then add eggs.
3. Mix dry ingredients and add milk.
4. Fold in blackberries and basil.
5. Bake for 18 minutes and top with blackberry frosting.

Snickerdoodle Cupcakes
Ingredients:

- 1 ½ cups flour
- 1 tsp baking powder
- ½ cup sugar
- ½ cup butter
- 2 eggs
- ½ cup milk
- 1 tsp cinnamon
- Cinnamon-sugar for topping

Instructions:

1. Preheat oven to 350°F.
2. Beat butter and sugar, then add eggs.
3. Mix dry ingredients and add milk.
4. Sprinkle tops with cinnamon-sugar before baking.
5. Bake for 18 minutes and top with cinnamon buttercream.

Butterbeer Cupcakes
Ingredients:

- 1 ½ cups flour
- 1 tsp baking powder
- ½ cup brown sugar
- ½ cup butter
- 2 eggs
- ½ cup cream soda
- ½ tsp butter extract

Instructions:

1. Preheat oven to 350°F.
2. Beat butter and sugar, then add eggs.
3. Mix dry ingredients and add cream soda and butter extract.
4. Bake for 18 minutes and top with butterscotch frosting.

Hazelnut Praline Cupcakes

Ingredients:

- 1 ½ cups flour
- 1 tsp baking powder
- ½ cup sugar
- ½ cup butter
- 2 eggs
- ½ cup milk
- ½ cup chopped hazelnuts
- ¼ cup caramel sauce

Instructions:

1. Preheat oven to 350°F.
2. Beat butter and sugar, then add eggs.
3. Mix dry ingredients and add milk.
4. Fold in hazelnuts and bake for 18 minutes.
5. Drizzle with caramel and top with praline crunch.

Raspberry Champagne Cupcakes
Ingredients:

- 1 ½ cups flour
- 1 tsp baking powder
- ½ cup sugar
- ½ cup butter
- 2 eggs
- ½ cup champagne
- ½ cup raspberries

Instructions:

1. Preheat oven to 350°F.
2. Beat butter and sugar, then add eggs.
3. Mix dry ingredients and add champagne.
4. Fold in raspberries and bake for 18 minutes.
5. Top with champagne frosting and edible gold dust.

Banana Foster Cupcakes

Ingredients:

- 1 ½ cups flour
- 1 tsp baking powder
- ½ cup brown sugar
- ½ cup butter
- 2 eggs
- ½ cup mashed banana
- 1 tbsp rum

Instructions:

1. Preheat oven to 350°F.
2. Beat butter and sugar, then add eggs.
3. Mix dry ingredients and add banana and rum.
4. Bake for 18 minutes.
5. Top with caramel rum frosting.

Chocolate Guinness Cupcakes
Ingredients:

- 1 ½ cups flour
- ½ cup cocoa powder
- 1 tsp baking powder
- ½ cup sugar
- ½ cup butter
- 2 eggs
- ½ cup Guinness stout

Instructions:

1. Preheat oven to 350°F.
2. Beat butter and sugar, then add eggs.
3. Mix dry ingredients and add Guinness.
4. Bake for 18 minutes and top with chocolate whiskey frosting.